Flourish!

Katesha Harrell

Flourish!

Katesha Harrell

SpeakLife
Publishing

Flourish!

Printed In The United States Of America
ISBN: 978-0615843681

Published By SPEAKLIFE PUBLISHING

**SpeakLife
Publishing**

"The Words I Speak, They Are Spirit And They Are Life."
John 6:63

P.O. Box 1791 Elizabeth City, NC 27906
1-888-596-3882
www.SpeakLifePublishing.com

"The Motivator" Lynetta Jordan, CEO

Unless otherwise noted, all scripture references are from the New King James version of the Bible.

Flourish!

Katesha Harrell

SpeakLife
Publishing

Flourish!

Published By SPEAKLIFE PUBLISHING

**SpeakLife
Publishing**

"The Words I Speak, They Are Spirit And They Are Life."
John 6:63

P.O. Box 1791   Elizabeth City, NC 27906
1-888-596-3882
www.SpeakLifePublishing.com

"The Motivator" Lynetta Jordan, CEO

Unless otherwise noted, all scripture references are from the New King James version of the Bible.

Flourish!

Table of Contents

INTRODUCTION

If this book has found its way into your hands, trust me, it is no coincidence. The reading of this book is an appointment with your destiny. It is time for you to flourish. No matter what life has brought your way, no matter what situation you were born into, no matter what you have done, no matter what injustice has been done to you, it is your time to flourish. No matter whose child you are, or even maybe whose child you thought you were, God has a plan and it is a plan that is for you to flourish.

You, dear reader are right at the brink of a new day. Destiny is propelling your spirit to take flight into new dimensions of life as you begin to understand just how God has uniquely designed you to flourish in life. You have permission to stand out as you blossom like the crocus flower leaving your desert state of life deserted forever. So with that being said, let us begin on this journey of flourishing with the light of the Lord shining upon us to help us grow.

Chapter One

What Does It Mean To Flourish?

As I began to ponder on the meaning of this word, I was lead to not only dig deeper, but to also share my findings. I specifically want to share with those of you who may have taken a detour in life or have simply found yourself stuck in a rotting environment. I pray that this book will be one of the many seeds that will propel your hope to sprout, grow exceedingly, and then bear produce for others to enjoy. Just as God's word, which is the seed that will never fail to bloom, states that we are to *"plant,*

1

water, and bear fruit."

Before I looked up the word flourish, I simply saw it as a pretty word meaning "to grow." It does indeed mean to grow; however, there is more.

FLOURISH

- To flourish means to grow vigorously
- to grow well or luxuriantly; thrive to do or fare well, prosper
- to be in a period of highest productivity, excellence, or influence to make bold, sweeping movements to wild, wave, or exhibit dramatically
- a dramatic or stylish movement
- to thrive or prosper
- to be at a peak of condition
- to be healthy
- to wave or cause to wave in the air with sweeping strokes (from glory to glory)
- to display or make a display
- to play a fanfare on a musical instrument
- to embellish writing, characters, with ornamental strokes
- to add decorations or embellishments to speech or writing
- obsolete word for **BLOSSOM**
- The use of movements(especially the hands) to communicate familiar or prearranged signals
- high flown **style**
- excessive use of verbal ornamentation
- **MELODY**

- grandiloquence, grandiosity, magniloquence, ornateness, rhetoric, thrive, expand, boom, revive-be brought back to life consciousness, or strength
- grow become larger, greater, bigger, expand, gain, luxuriate.
- to make steady **progress** at a high point in one's career or reach a high point in historical significance or importance
- change, stare, turn-undergo a **TRANSFORMATION** or a change of a position or action
- Strong, energetic, and active in mind or body; robust.
- Marked by or done with force and energy.

Once you have accepted Jesus Christ as your Lord and Savior something should enter your very vital organs that enables you to live your new life in a vigorous way. That something is the Holy Spirit. The Holy Spirit will enable you to live in a manner that is marked with supernatural energy. Am I saying that you will never grow tired or weary? Absolutely not!

The key is that when you are living your life connected to the vine of Jesus Christ you will know where it is that your help comes from. You will consistently continue to flourish as you lean on Him for the mental and physical energy needed to sustain you in your arena of life.

Growing vigorously in Christ also means growing in a healthy manner. Christians often quote the scriptures, *"By your stripes we were healed" (Isaiah 53:5) and "For God so loved the world that He gave His only son to die on the cross" (John 3: 16)* . But I heard a minister say something that will remain with me for a lifetime. Did you realize that when Jesus was taking those stripes He was also bearing mental anguish so that we would not have to? As a society we focus so much on our physical health that we sometimes forget to sustain our mental and spiritual wellbeing as well.

Jesus bore that mental and psychological agony of abuse, pain, neglect, rejection, humiliation, and torment so that when we gave Him our lives we would not have to undergo that pain. Just imagine for a moment the mental torment that Jesus bore. By no means am I belittling the physical pain that He endured. But sometimes I think we forget about the psychological pressure that people in pain are under. Jesus was whipped, beaten, bruised, battered and torn.

He was neglected by the majority of the world that He was enduring this pain for. He was openly rejected by some of the same people that He poured His very essence into. I can only imagine the amount of humiliation that He must of felt having to have all of these erogenous acts performed right in His natural mother's face.

Have you ever found yourself in a moment of your life that hurt so badly it felt like the *Never Ending Story*? Perhaps it's a relationship gone awry or a position you know you were qualified for, but simply overlooked. Maybe you were conned out of your life savings by a crooked business partner or perhaps even your virginity. Perhaps you were left to raise your family alone, or maybe you did everything correctly and you are still alone. God knows your story.

Jesus knew you were going to have this story. Jesus knew that we were not going to be able to handle this mental anguish alone. That is why He bore the physical, mental, and psychological pain on that Old Rugged Cross.

He could have stopped it all at any point but he endured it all so that we would not have to. We literally have the ability today to say, "Jesus this is your pain and your problem. I give this mental confusion and despair for you to handle and do with as you please. It is not for me to carry, fix, worry, or ponder any longer." Go ahead let Him be the gentleman that he is and carry all those bags for you. He is strong enough; let your mind be free from all of those entanglements today.

I am a woman that is striving to flourish vigorously. I want to live a life full of supernatural energy in body, mind, and spirit. In other words, God wants not only me but you as well to flourish in a whole manner. Part of our growth as a whole Christian is to also ensure that our environments are healthy. Our home, school, office, and church environments must be full of health and vitality in order for us to flourish in life and in the kingdom of God. God desires for us to prosper and be in good health. He also wants us to do our part to live at peace with man. Sometimes it can be difficult for our environments to be healthy when we live with or work with mentally or spiritually unhealthy people. However, I believe this is where we sometimes experience the most tremendous growth in our Christian walk. This is when we learn to depend on the Holy Spirit to keep us healthy, after we have done our part to remain at peace in these various environments.

Another definition of flourish is to grow well or luxuriantly; thrive to do or fare well, prosper. It also means to grow with vigor and great abundance, characterized by richness and extravagance. In the Christian community you will hear a lot about spiritual growth or growing in Christ. What is meant by this is simply that we should mature or grow in our knowledge, strength, and confidence of who God is and how our everyday decisions are affected by this growing knowledge.

Again, to grow well I believe is all about our environment. Think about a plant. For years I watched my grandmother care for her plants. I watched one plant turn into about five or more plants. This always amazed me. I believe that when we grow well, we can positively affect the growth of others. My grandmother made sure the plants had just enough water, and just enough sunlight. When she noticed that it needed more room to grow she would go ahead and re-pot it into a larger container.

She also knew the best soil to use for certain types of

plants. My grandmother did not get upset often, but if you wanted to make her mad, just act like you were going to upset the environment of one of those plants. Some would say she had a green thumb. I say she took the time and effort to learn what worked to achieve and maintain the lush and extravagant growth of her plants.

Just as it takes careful tenacity to have a plant to grow well, how much more energy should we take to ensure that we flourish in life? Both Christian and Secular research proves that our environment either positively or negatively affects our growth. We must protect our eye gate, ear gate, and of course the little member of our body that James warns us of- our tongue. *"Even so the tongue is a little member and boasts great things. See how great a forest a little fire kindles"* (James 3:5).

What we see forms an image of what our brains will begin to think we should emulate. Whatever information we hear our brains will begin to believe and repeat. It's as if our subconscious is flooded with this information and overrides what we know in our inner man to be the concrete truth. And of course preachers, teachers and everyone always says you get what you speak. What we allow ourselves to believe as truth and speak from our mouths will come to pass. Scripture says *"Out of the abundance of the heart the mouth speaks" (Matthew 12:34)* and *"Whoever says to this mountain, Be removed and be cast into the sea, and does not doubt in his heart, but believes that those things he says will be done, he will have whatever he asks" (Mark 11:23).*

3 John 1:2 states, *"Beloved, I wish that thou mayest prosper and be in good health, even as thy soul prospereth."* Jeremiah 29:11 states, *"For I know the thoughts that I think toward you says the Lord, plans to prosper you and not to harm you, to give you a hope and a future."* Friends, I am here to declare to you on this day that the Lord only has your best interest in mind. Some of you are so hard-hearted and downtrodden due to past experiences with unhealthy people that it is difficult for you to believe that even the Almighty God has your best interest at heart. God desires to see you prosper in every area of your life.

Some of you may be in a place of your life where prosperity seems unachievable. My friend this is where

God specializes. In the Bible a woman that was caught in the act of adultery was pardoned by Jesus as he told those on looking, sneering, mocking, whispering to cast the first stone if they were without sin. The woman at the well with multiple relationships was told by Jesus himself to go and sin no more. A pregnant fourteen-year-old was scared, embarrassed, confused, and not expected to achieve her life's goals and dreams is now the mother of a nineteen year old who is doing as she pleases in life. God's desire is for you to prosper in life.

I hear a lot of ministers on television bash prosperity ministers, as they say this does not teach a balanced Christian lifestyle. I say if you're already down in spirit, in finance, in health, in friends, in joy, or in peace then you might as well go ahead and allow the living spirit of God to fill you and prosper you in every area of your life. God himself has given us permission to grow well in our Christian walk with the Lord.

When I saw that to flourish meant to be in a period of highest productivity I really began to get excited. Life with Christ is a journey. It is the journey of your life where you achieve the highest level of success. As you grow in your knowledge of the Lord in your journey, you also grow in your knowledge of yourself. There are no limits of as to how much you are capable of producing in your life. You are in competition with no one, and as supermodel Kathy Ireland stated, *"Success is breaking your own glass ceiling."*

When you begin to break free from and flourish in the areas of your life that once upon a time simply felt like a dream, this is when you know you are moving forward with productivity. For some reason when I hear the word productivity all I can think about is the business world. If the business is not producing anything profitable the owner will gather information needed to work out a new plan for success. Well I believe it is time for us to examine our lives. If there is an area without any production we must make a new plan and then work the plan.

The thing I love about God the most is that you do not have to be superwoman to be in high productivity. All you have to do is obey God in whatever season of life you are in. If you are a wife, mother, full time employee, and an entrepreneur, go on sister and flourish. If you are a single woman waiting for your husband you too are flourishing. If you are in a shelter believing God for your next step in life you too are flourishing in your faith of trusting God. If you are a single parent with a troubled teen do not sit around and beat yourself up for what could have, should have, or would have been. The best thing you can do is be bold and dare to flourish even in this season of your life.

It is in these hard times of our lives where we excel in our love, joy, peace, faith, long-suffering, mercy, and patience. These are the moments of life where we make bold sweeping movements that cause us to have a tremendous amount of influence on others. A lot of times we think we have to have a lot of things to have a lot of influence. In order to have a lot of influence all we need is a lot of love.

The most bold and exciting movement that you can make is to allow yourself to accept and acknowledge the love of Father God. Once you begin to experience and dramatically display His love your life will continually be in a period of high productivity and influence.

To flourish means to wave or cause to wave in the air

with sweeping strokes and to display or make a display. The Bible instructs us to lift up our hands in the sanctuary and bless the lord (*Psalm 134: 2*). When you are living your life in the presence of God your hands will automatically go up as you concentrate on Him. Your hands will wave in praise, adoration, worship, and surrender.

Our lives are in a constant state of a sweeping motion as we travel from glory to glory in our journey with the Lord. We are on display for Christ as our lives flourish. He takes our mess and turns it into a message that reveals His glory. David made a big mess, but once he repented and saw the error of his ways God surely used his life story as one of the major messages in the Bible. I am able to effectively minister to women today because of the pain I have experienced due to poor choices in life.

I have a burning desire to halt young ladies from going through any of the anxiety and turmoil that negatively impacted my life. I also have a desire to see women who have detoured get back on the right track. The important thing to remember is that it really does not matter what others think or say about you; He is the potter and you are the clay. You my dear are on display.

The next definition of flourish is to embellish writing, characters, with ornamental strokes and to add decorations or embellishments to speech or writing. I take this to simply inform us that God has strategically gifted us in so many different areas. When God's anointing is on you in your area of gifting or expertise you will certainly flourish in life. We are God's workmanship; He has fearfully and wonderfully made us in His image and likeness. Therefore we are awesome in our gifting as God has created us in His awesomeness.

Whatever we do in life; God desires for us to do it with bells on so to speak. In John Bevere's teaching on Relentless he stresses and brings to our attention how we as the body of Christ are given the ability to do anything that we do ten times better than people without faith. Not for our own vain glory but simply to exemplify Christ and show His power and presence to a lost and dying world.

Smith Wigglesworth was born unable to speak, today he is well known as a hero in the faith for not only reading, writing, and speaking but also for the legacy of signs and wonders he operated in. Once God healed him he was determined to embellish the world with what great faith in God could produce. God performed ornamental miracles through his ministry.

Did you know that Smith Wigglesworth's wife interceded for her husband to learn to read and write as she ministered to others? I see her as a woman who flourished in her ministry as she believed God for the success of her husband. God surely rewarded her by allowing her husband's name to prosper. For the Bible states, *"Better is a good name than all the riches in the world" (Proverbs 22:1).*

Bishop Paul Morton is a popular pastor, teacher, recording artist, and writer today. What most people do not know about him is that he is married to a woman who has dared to flourish in life. She was one of the first women to preach in a Baptist church has authored six books, and is a current owner of a spa built on Godly principals. What I found to be her most ornamental act was that she was able to use some of her own funds to help get their church back up and running after Hurricane Katrina. Wow, imagine the number of lives that have now been impacted by her sheer obedience to God.

Just wonder for a few moments just how God desires to decorate the world with your capabilities. Sometimes I think we sink down in fear when we do not think we are good enough, educated enough, or well off enough. Always remember God sees you as the you He created. He created you with just enough of everything you need to leave your thumbprint in the world.

Kris Radish is an American novelist who writes fiction stories about women who come from not so fiction situations. He recently wrote an article for Writers Digest titled "An *Audience of One.*" In his article he expresses how his life was forever impacted by one inspirational woman. Radish was featured as a guest speaker for a book signing, which is great promotion for an author. The problem was only one guest showed.

Radish said the owner asked him if he was interested in rescheduling as the turnout was not so great. The guest was a woman in shabby clothing. He went on to perform his lecture and talk session just as if there was a full house. In the talk session he learned that this woman used to be homeless and live behind this very book store.

16

She stated that she used to watch authors such as Radish come and go.

This woman had made it one of her life's goals to come and sit in on one. That particular day just happened to be the day she built up the nerve to come. Needless to say this author said if his books only helped this one person it was all worth it.

Whether your gift is writing, teaching, singing, preaching, giving, painting, or helping it can be used to bless the world. God spent his time imparting into you some sort of ornamental gifting. It should be our duty and joy to see to it that we discover it and use it to bless Him and others in a way that only we can.

The scripture, *"I can do all things through Christ that strengthens me" (Philippians 4:13)* comes to my mind with the next definition of flourish. Flourish also means to make steady progress at a high point in one's career or reach a high point in historical significance. Life with Christ will certainly push you to flourish in your career to the point that your thumbprint is left in your field.

I think the key point here is not that we are perfect but simply that we are constantly progressing not only in our walk with Christ but also in our career. The Bible says that we are constantly growing from glory to glory. There is always room for improvement no matter what level we are on. As a new creature in Christ we do not strive to be world changers or history makers, we just are as we are obedient to the spirit of Christ.

Even as I am speaking to you about flourishing, I hesitated on the completion of launching this book to you because my life is not perfect, my words are not perfect. However, I know that I serve a perfect God and that if He indeed graced me with the opportunity to speak to you though my writing then his perfect touch is on this book to touch your heart in a perfect manner. And I further encourage you to stop waiting for that perfect moment to be obedient to what you know is right. Just go for it and do what the Lord has spoken to you to do. In the Bible the prophet Nathan gave David this same advice- to just do it! 2nd Samuel 7:17 states, *"Go do all that is in all your heart for the Lord is with you."*

After studying this scripture three years ago I had a dream that I was reading a handwritten note. The letter was addressed to me with Dear Katesha. The first line of the letter read, *"Pursue all of your life's goals and dreams."* The rest of the letter faded up until the end which stated Love, God. There are no words to express how much that dream prompted me to begin a beautiful journey in writing, worshiping, teaching, and so much more. But the most beautiful part of it all is that God gave me a desire to see other women believe in their dreams again as well.

Just as the crocus flower blooms you to are destined to flourish in your arena of life. As a stay at home mom you have the perfect ability to place your blessed hands on every aspect of your child's life. You have the perfect ability to pour into your child or children on a daily basis the proper nourishment that they need to grow into prosperous individuals. Some of you may be thinking Katesha you do not know what I went through as a kid, Katesha I do not think I can handle this responsibility, or Katesha I have waited so long to be a mother that I am afraid of God punishing me if I do not do everything correctly. If I were there with you I would tell you, *"You can do all things through Christ that strengthens you."* Now go forth and be the mom that God destined you to be. And if you are waiting to be a mom just hold fast because your child is so special that God is still shaping, making, and molding your child in heaven before he/she is placed in your womb. Or perhaps God has destiny for your child at an appointed time in history, so continue your expecting wait time.

As professional women in the workplace you may feel ....alone. By this I mean you went to college, earned you degree, have your own home, and you are surrounded by successful people; however you don't feel the sense of fulfillment that you always thought you would when you landed that six figure promotion. There's still a yearning coming from deep inside you that you even figured out that no man can fill.

I believe that a part of your steady growth in your career has just as much to do with your attitude as it does your altitude. As you flourish in your career path with God on your side you will enrich lives along the way. You will find a way to propel others as you rise. Your ultimate goal will be to share God's love, joy, and peace as you reach promotion. This will make you a history maker; not only will you be the chic with the corner office, you'll be the chic that is a part of something bigger than herself and obtained the corner office.

Perhaps you are homeless or in a shelter reading this book now and you see absolutely no way out of your current situation. You see the word promotion and your heart sinks because you are in your situation now because of a demotion. You loved God with all your heart and you were still the first to be let go from your corporation. You sowed faithfully into the kingdom of God and your husband still left you with every penny you had in the bank. Or perhaps you just gave that man every ounce of love and care and devotion you had inside of you and he still left you pregnant and all.

As I write this portion of this book, I am in a ferry for two and a half hours to stay on a sixteen mile island all-expense paid including breakfast, lunch and dinner for five days. All I have to do is wake up every day surrounded by the ocean and learn strategies and techniques to improve my skill with other colleagues from across the state. Now excuse me for a moment while I get my praise on for God allowing me to flourish in my career!

I can praise God right now because I remember when...... Ten years ago I remember when I was living in low income housing with a nine year old, six year old, five year old, and four year old. The apartment was roach infested, needed various things repaired, and I was praying to God every day for tuition and strength to complete my university education.

I remember when every month that I paid my rent I would politely ask for a date that my apartment would be tended to. I was always told a date and of course you know something always came up or they were waiting for the state to send funds for them to take care of my place. When I obtained my first teaching position my landlord's son just so happened to be one of my students. Now I was being given dates for my apartment to be fixed without my asking. But I must tell you, it was too late we moved into a beautiful home that had only been built for two years with our own backyard.

Can you think of something that you can stop and praise God for right now? If not then simply give him a yet praise. Praise him in spite of your situation. Or better yet give him a prophetic praise. Praise him in advance. I am praising Him now in advance, months before this book is even sent to a publisher. I am praising him for allowing you to read this book and I know that you are flourishing.

I do not think it's an accident that you bought, borrowed, or were given this book. I am here just to hold your hand with words of comfort and encouragement. You can do it! You can make it! God is for you not against you! You will progress in life! Go ahead and cry if need be but then clean up dust off and dream again!

It should not be a surprise that to flourish also means to change, turn, or undergo a transformation. The Bible simply states, *"If any man be in Christ he is a new creature, Old things are passed away" (2 Corinthians 5:17).* For one moment just stop to think about a beautiful flower in full bloom. Well it did not always look that awesome. It took a little time, rain, and rays of sun for that flower to blossom. It is the same way with us, as we continue to grow with the Lord. He is continually transforming us into the real authentic version of who he created us to be. He will continue to finish the good work in you that he has begun as you grow into full bloom. *"Being confident of this very thing, that He who has begun a good work in you will complete it until the day of Jesus Christ"* (Philippians 1:6).

I believe that God will transform the way we think as we continue to read his word. He will continue to change the way we see ourselves and others. He will transform, anoint, and redeem us from our filthy past so that we can be change agents in the lives of others. God has certainly changed my way of life. I used to be very uncomfortable speaking my mind even when I knew I was right. I used to believe that my voice did not matter. I used to believe that I was unattractive and untalented. To sum it up I just used to believe that I was not good enough.

Well as I really began to listen to, read, and adhere to the word of God, I finally realized that God created me. It is really as simple as that. God created you. He took the time to carefully place the number of hairs on your head and determine which X and Y chromosomes you were to genetically inherit. He created you with the end in mind. He knew what type of flower you would blossom into being after you went through your transformation state.

How many women do you know that stopped right in the middle of their transformation stage by holding on to anger, bitterness, hurt, or trauma? They seem to be stuck in: she stole my boyfriend, she took my lead in the church choir, my husband had a baby on me. I believe that it breaks God's heart when we do this. Just as it breaks our heart when we do all we can to raise a child to the best of our ability with affirmations, structure, guidance, and love just to watch them run away from their calling and waste their God-given potential. How much more must it ache the very heart of our Father God when he watches us stop our blooming process by holding on to the agony and contempt we sometimes feel?

No matter how deep the scar of your past there is a place where you can go for healing. That place is into the presence of God. In his presence there is a deep inner healing that can penetrate into the crevices of our soul. Since our soul consists of our mind, will, and emotions that is where we need him to be. He can send healing into the crevice of our mind from continuing to repeat all of the negative comments that we have ever heard about ourselves.

He can send healing into the crevice of our will of being sluggish from fighting so hard to pretend to smile like everything is alright when in reality we feel like "One more day of this mess and I am going to go off!" He can send healing into the crevice of our emotions from feeling the sting of the past every time we hear a person's name or see their face, or are just simply reminded of the person who wronged us in some type of way.

The Bible simply states, *"You did run well, who did hinder you that you should not obey the truth" (Galatians 5:7)*. I encourage you to strive to hear the words, *"Well done thy good and faithful servant"* instead. I have always thought of this verse as something I must physically do to help build God's kingdom. But just stop for a moment and think what if all we need to do is forgive our sister or brother or maybe even our mother or father for some act that they performed against us or to us that has caused us to hold offense in our hearts to hear him say these words, *"Well done."*

A synonym for flourish is melody. I studied music in

my adolescent years, and everyone feels privileged when they are given the opportunity to lead in the melody. Without the melody, there is no song. Without the melody there is nothing for the listener to connect with or retain. Without the very melody of the song there would be no passion or emotion evoked inside of the listener.

Without the melody it would simply just be noise, or a *"tinkling cymbal"*(1 *Corinthians* 13:1) without any love or clarity behind it. The melody is what connects all other parts of the song, just as love connects our souls. Without a melody there would be no harmony or unity. The Bible states, *"How good and sweet it is for brethren to dwell together in unity" (Psalm 133:1).* Psalm 133:3 further states that this is the place where God will command a blessing. If the melody is not intact then it is completely difficult for the audience to grasp the meaning or message that the song is attempting to display. Without the love of God you cannot display God's presence, peace, or power.

What message is your life displaying? Does your life display the grandiloquence, which is another synonym for flourish, of God's grace and mercy? Or does your life display the gates of hell that you have either been too afraid to face and displace or just simply did not know that you were not created to remain in those gates of captivity.

I call these blockages in life gates, some call them glass ceilings. Basically they are the unspoken rules that we sometimes live our lives based on as a result of our upbringing. In the Education Profession there is a book entitled, *Understanding the Framework of Poverty* by Ruby Payne.

Basically her book proves that poverty has nothing to do with how much money you have or don't have, but it has everything to do with how many glass ceilings or gates are you willing to knock down. How you treat people, the way you behave at the dinner table, understanding principles such as tithing and saving are all aspects of middle and upper class. Your ability to surround yourself with positive people or let bad ones go are also a part of the hidden rules of the middle and upper class.

Ladies you must begin to believe that God has a plan for your life. You must begin to believe that he wants to do new things in you and through you. He loves you just as you are. He loves you even when it seems as if the seeds of harvest are deep inside your soul. But my prayer is that as you continue to read this book you begin to come into full bloom and flourish. I desire for you to flourish in your mind, body, and soul.

Chapter 2

Why Should I Flourish?

Of course there are many reasons of as to why a person should choose to flourish or choose life over death so to speak (Deuteronomy 30:15). But what it all boils down to is that we should desire to flourish so that we can bless God and others. We were created to worship God with the very breath that he breathed into us. No one has the ability to bloom into the creation that God destined for you to be just as no one can worship God in the same manner as you can. You have your own thumbprint to leave behind literally and figuratively.

There are plants here on earth that only bloom once a

year or once in a lifetime. Their owners will wait patiently and prepare for the day that the plant will bloom. The only way these plants do not bloom on schedule is if some environmental process has completely destroyed the roots. I believe that God is waiting for the day of our blooming arrival. When I say blooming arrival I mean the day that we accept Him in our hearts, the day that we have that worship experience with Him that brings us into a deeper relationship.

All of these budding moments in His presence bring us into full bloom. In full bloom is when we can begin to have a major impact on the lives of others. Other people see themselves stuck in between the walls that they witnessed you tear down from your life and begin to believe that God can do it for them too. You can begin to share your testimony with others and their lives will be radically changed just because you had the courage to tell the truth and shame the devil. Your truth has the potential to become someone's HOPE!

A lot of times we will not share our testimonies because we feel ashamed. I beg to differ; your testimony shames the devil because it sets captives free. There is freedom in flourishing in life. There is freedom in living the life that was meant and predestined for you. Just because your parents, uncle, cousin, and best friend choose to live their lives on the island of hopelessness and despair does not mean that you have to. You have the ability to accomplish every goal and dream that God plants inside your heart.

You should flourish in your life to inwardly and outwardly reflect the glory of the Lord. *"May the glory of God's face shine on you"* (Numbers *6:25)* as you continue to fight until injustice and shame are gone from your life. I pray that right now in this moment all shame and condemnation be broken off of you. Shame from your past or even from your present circumstance hinders you no more.

Some of you are successful in your professional life, but you come home every night and battle with thoughts of shame from hurtful things that have happened in your past. Your trust issues prevent you from having faith in even the most humble and gentle people in your life. Having your guard up with a wall of protection around your heart has added to your exuberant career; however, it has kept you from experiencing lasting relationships and more importantly it has kept you from experiencing the genuine love of the Father. Your walls of shame, embarrassment, and defeat in this area of your life have hardened your heart. But I am here to tell you that the Bible says that God holds the heart of the king in his hands.

That means that your heart is not too hard or too heavy for him to hold. That means you do not have to try to figure out how someone could do that to you or why someone would do that to you all on your own. God is holding your heart in His hands which even means that you no longer have to live in the shame of your past. I prophesy that as you continue to read these words your heart will be softened in his hands. And as your heart softens towards the Father, your heart will soften towards your family, friends, neighbors, and co-workers.

As God softens your heart the most amazing thing takes place. You look on others with newness. You begin to see you are not the only one dealing with your issue and that you're not the only one who has already dealt with that issue. You actually begin to see that you really have nothing to be ashamed of. Jesus hung, bled, and died so that you could be free from all guilt, hurt, pain, sickness, disease, and shame.

Some of you are holding on to shame in order to punish yourself for something that you have done wrong. It is almost as if you have reasoned with yourself that, yes, God loves me; yes, I am saved. But I cheated on my spouse, drank alcohol while I was pregnant, gave my baby away for adoption when I got pregnant in college, ignored my best friend's plea for help before she committed suicide because I was jealous of her seemingly perfect life. So you kept living, but you kept living with an ounce of shame. Trade that shame for the joy of the Lord today.

As you pursue to flourish in life by letting go of all your shame you gain an ability to have an impact on others with your words and actions. Others will begin to see you outwardly as you interact with your spouse, children, or coworkers and will desire whatever it is that has allowed you to take a blow and continue to sow into the lives of others. The shame is no longer on you, but is now back on the devil as light is shinning on the truths of your heart. *"Arise; shine; for your light has come: and the glory of the Lord is risen upon you. The Lord will arise over you, and His glory will be seen upon you"* (Isaiah 60:1-2).

Perhaps the enemy has spoken to you and told you that your chance to flourish has passed you by. Maybe you struggle with thoughts of unachieved dreams as you have progressed in age. You have raised your children and catered to your husband only to be left with a sense of hollowness. Well do not worry, do not fret. There is a yet blessing waiting for you.

The image of a perfect gentlemen dressed in a tux with a perfect single red rose comes to my mind for you. He, the Holy Spirit, is awaiting your acceptance to His invitation of dancing with you. He wants to dance with you and over your life. But the Holy Spirit being the gentleman that he is will simply lead you in the steps of your life just as a perfect gentleman leads the dance steps of his lady dancing partner.

Come into a new partnership with Him. Step into a partnership with Christ where He does all the leading and directing. All you have to do is accept his invitation to be his dance partner. You never know what type of dance you'll be doing or what type of music will be playing. But you will know that it will be just for you!

Just as every flower bud in its own time and season you will flourish at your own rate. As others observe your dance in life they too will want to accept the invitation to dance with the king, the gentleman, the giver of life. Your children, whether young or adult will desire to join you on the dance floor. Your husband will desire to join in on your dance as you pursue your life's goals. Before you know it your dance floor will be filled with the people that you have influenced by allowing the Holy Spirit to capture your attention and order your steps.

The Bible states that, *"The steps of a good man are ordered by the Lord: and he delighteth in his way"* (Psalm 37:22). When we order our food from a restaurant we expect it to be prepared just so. Well I believe that as God orders our steps, He will not allow us to settle in life for anything other than what He has ordered or ordained for us to be. So if you are dealing with feelings of hollowness and exhaustion then perhaps it is time for you to seek what the father has prepared for you and flourish in life.

Some of you are carrying shame because of your present situations. You're in a season of your life where you realize that you did not care for your child in the most proper manner. You realize the hurt and agony you caused another family member to experience by having a relationship with a married man. The good news is you have acknowledged that what you did was wrong. Now let go of the shame, move on, and encourage someone else that still has a chance to bypass the detour you took in life.

Perhaps you are a broken women with a tragic past. Maybe your past is so horrific it has left you hostile, destitute, empty, alone, or in poverty. Maybe there is so much shame on you that you lost sight of your future. You simply exist day to day in your home all alone or in a shelter without a single soul to be concerned about you.

I say you are the perfect candidate to make a dramatic move toward walking in your destiny. No matter what life has thrown your way do not give into the enemy by believing this is your lot in life and you must remain. Lot's wife in the Bible was told to move and not look back. She had such a connection with what was and what had been that she did just as she was told not to. She looked back. Her disobedience caused her to turn into a pillar of salt. She never got a chance to experience new life with her husband Lot because she looked back, and became a pillar of salt (Genesis 19:26).

Dear reader, Don't look back! Don't turn into a pillar of salt; be the salt. The Bible states that we are to be the salt of the earth. *"You are the salt of the earth, but if salt has lost its taste (its strength, its quality), how can its saltiness be restored? It is not good for anything any longer but to be thrown out and trodden underfoot by men. You are the light of the world. A city set on a hill that cannot be hidden"* (Matthew 5:13-14 Amplified Bible).

Don't turn into a pillar of salt with a hateful attitude towards your loved ones. Don't turn into a pillar of salt and leave your family with a marred image of who you really were inside. Press on in life to be the perfect flavor that your family and community needs. Press on in life and flourish to leave your thumbprint in the world.

Chapter 3

How Can I Flourish?

Now that you know what flourish means and why it is so important to flourish in life you may be wondering how can I flourish? Once you have made up in your mind that you can no longer live your life without being the melody that you long to hear, your life will begin to blossom.

I believe that you can start by reconnecting with your dreams. Anything that you have always dreamt of doing you can do it. You can do it because God is the dream giver. God will not give you a dream without giving you the grace to accomplish it. You must trust that God can see your dream through, no matter what your current circumstance.

The Bible states *"Trust in the Lord with all thine heart. Lean not unto thine own understanding and in all thy ways acknowledge Him and He will direct your paths"* (Proverbs 3: 5-6). When I was in college, there was an eighty-year old man that was in school as well. Several people zoomed by him on the way to class, others stared at him to try to make him feel out of place. However, he continued to come to each class every day walking at his own pace. He stated one day that it was always his dream to earn a college degree, but when he was younger he had to go to work. This man did not give up on his dream.

The famous Clark sisters are living out not only their own personal dreams but also the dreams of their late mother, Dr. Mattie Moss-Clark. Dorinda Clark, one of the Clark sisters, stated during an interview that their mother would wake them up in the middle of the night to practice parts to songs that she was writing for other famous gospel singers. Now at the time Dorinda and her siblings probably did not really appreciate their mother's enthusiasm for music ministry. But today, these powerful sisters: Jacky, Twinkie, Dorinda, and Karen are anointed women of God that have been able to proceed through many open doors in life because their mother dared to dream. According to Dorinda's website, Dr. Mattie Moss-Clark is well known today for being the first person to *"commit the sounds of a choir to a record"* in 1958. She is also well known today for being the first to separate parts into soprano, alto, and tenor. Not only did she dare to dream but she also dared to instill her passion to dream into her children. Now we listen to music that was written by this remarkable woman. We also listen to music written, produced, composed, and sang by her children and grandchildren.

What would happen in your life, in the life of your children, or even in the life of those around you if you dared to dream again? Langston Hughes wrote a poem entitled, *"Dare to Dream."* The poem is as follows:

Hold fast to dreams,
For if dreams die
Life is a broken-winged bird,

That cannot fly.

You must reconnect with the vision of your dream that lies deep within you in order to flourish. You were not meant to remain low in life. You were not meant to live your life as if you cannot soar in achieving your dreams due to life's circumstances. Take some time to ask yourself what should you be doing or what would you like to do with your life? It is not too late; there is still time.

If Abraham and Sarah could reproduce in their latter years of life then surely you and I can still birth the destiny that lies within. You never know whose destiny is locked inside your lions. For example, you are reading this book. This book was birthed from me as I gained a passion to encourage women as I went through a time of tremendous emotional pain as a parent and as a wife. However, I dared to believe that I can still achieve my dreams. Hopefully this book allows you to realize there is still hope for your future.

Some years ago I had a dream of becoming a teacher. For me this dream seemed almost unachievable as I had not yet completed my Bachelor's degree. I was a wife and a mother of four. I dared to believe that it was my calling and a portion of my destiny to achieve this goal. When I dropped out of college at age 20 my GPA dropped tremendously as I did not go through the proper procedures and received all F's for a semester. My GPA was so low that I was told by the education department that I should change my major because there was no chance of getting accepted into the Teacher Education Department.

The Bible states that, *"All things work together for the good of those that love him"* *(Romans 8:28).* Even the discouragement of being denied worked out for my good. It led to me double majoring. God will give you double for your trouble, just as he did for Job. I changed my major to English-which is my passion- and took as many courses I could each semester. After two semesters of receiving all A's my GPA was up high enough to be accepted into the Teacher Education program, so I ended up with a Bachelor's in English and a Bachelor's in Education.

This was only the beginning. My last semester of school was supposed to be an unpaid internship where you work under another teacher. Well I really believed God for employment and most people thought it was impossible. I will never forget it was August of 2008 and school was going to begin in one week. I had been on interview after interview the entire summer. I even interviewed in school districts that were up to a one hour drive away.

But on this particular summer week I woke up every single morning, Monday thru Friday and got dressed just as if I was going to work. Each day I simply thanked God that I had found favor with a school system and that employment was around the corner. My faith soared as on that Friday at 4:30pm a school district only a few minutes outside of town called and offered me a two week substitution position. All I had to do was show up on the first day of school to complete paper work.

Now here is the most intense part of the testimony. The Central Office said they heard about me from another interview that I previously had with a neighboring school district. The school district that employed me never even interviewed me! My friend, one employer may not hire you or might let you go, but God always has a ram in the bush that is just right for you in His perfect timing.

After two weeks of working as a substitute, the principal asked me if I would stay eight more weeks. As the eight weeks came to a halt, the principal then asked me to remain for the remainder of the school year as a long-term substitute teacher. This became an issue as the university said that it was a law that intern teachers could not be receiving pay. The school system fought for me as they went back and forth as I simply showed up for work every day.

The Lord will fight your battles for you. All we have to do is keep doing what we are supposed to do day after day until breakthrough comes our way. Eventually the head of the Education Department from the university set up a meeting for me to come to his office. His exact words were, "Katesha, you have really made an impression working with this county. I do not even know how we are working this out, but you get to keep your pay, gain experience and earn your degree. Thank you for representing our university well." Today I work in a school system two hours away where his daughter is my principal. Need I say God gave me the grace and patience to achieve the dream that I had of becoming a teacher.

The funny thing is I have never shared this testimony with my principal. To my knowledge she has no idea that her father had to witness me going from being denied acceptance into the Teacher Education program to representing the Teacher Education program of that same university with excellence; so much so that the chancellor himself came to my classroom to visit one of my classes for a day.

Before all of this came to pass I had to make a decision to pay the price of my dream. John Maxwell stated, *"The dream is free but the journey is not."* Friends, it took a lot of time, sacrifices, energy, and just plan work to achieve this dream. I had to complete the same assignments as all the other students, no excuses. What made me different from the other students is that I had a family that still needed my attention and I still had a desire to be committed to my church family. But when you have a desire to flourish God will allow you to prosper. The Bible states, *"When you delight yourself in the Lord he will give you the desires of your heart"*

(Psalm 37:4).

You can flourish in life by simply doing what you were called to do; or performing whatever task is required of you in whatever season of life you are in. Take a spiritual gift inventory to see if you can discover a hidden talent you possess that you did not know of or that you perhaps forgot you even enjoyed. Take up a new class or hobby that is totally out of the box for your personality type just to see if you would enjoy it. We are reminded in the Bible to *"Neglect not the gifts that are inside of us,"* *"To stir up our gifts,"* and that *"Our gifts will make room for us"* (1 Timothy 4:14, II Timothy 1:6, Proverbs 18:16).

Each and every one of you has a creative gifting or talent that can be used to the glory of the Lord. Some of you can create a center piece that can carry such a creative anointing that your guests will feel the tangible presence of God while they remain in your home. Some of you have a unique gifting to work with youth. For some reason the youth just simply soak up every word you have to say. Some of you have an awesome gift of administration. You walk into a chaotic situation and delegate an action plan so elaborate that everyone cooperates and things begin to run smoothly within minutes. Some of you have such a gifting of wise counsel that even in the shelter people are drawn to you to communicate their hardships with you and ask for your advice. You give it to them but in the back of your mind your thinking, "Excuse me, do you not realize that obviously I have some issues of my own because I am right here in this shelter with you?"

Some of you have literally given the shirts and skirts right off you back. Did you know that this too is one of the spiritual gifts that only God can fill an individual with. Not everyone is so willing to give at the sight of a need. I thank God for those of you who possess this precious gift.

I remember when I was in a grocery store not too far from my home. I had about five items to check out. They were simply the basic grocery needs along with a couple of cans of formula. Well I had to leave a few items behind as the total was bit more than what I expected. As I was strapping one of my children into their car seat, this lady came running out of the store with the items I had left behind. She said she wanted to purchase them for me because she did not forget what it was like to choose between formula and food.

You would have thought this woman had placed a winning lottery ticket in my hand. I was so overjoyed not so much with the food, but with the fact that God had not forgotten me. This act of giving showed me that I was high on God's priority list even though I felt like I was at a low place in my life.

1 Corinthians 12

4 Now there are distinctive varieties and distributions of endowments (gifts, extraordinary powers distinguishing certain Christians, due to the power of divine grace operating in their souls by the Holy Spirit) and they vary, but the [Holy] Spirit remains the same.

5 And there are distinctive varieties of service and administration, but it is the same Lord [Who is served].

6 And there are distinctive varieties of operation [of working to accomplish things], but it is the same God Who inspires and energizes them all in all.

7 But to each one is given the manifestation of the [Holy] Spirit [the evidence, the spiritual illumination of the Spirit] for good and profit.

8 To one is given in and through the [Holy] Spirit [the power to speak] a message of wisdom, and to another [the power to express] a word of knowledge

and understanding according to the same [Holy] Spirit;

9 To another [wonder-working] faith by the same [Holy] Spirit, to another the extraordinary powers of healing by the one Spirit;

10 To another the working of miracles, to another prophetic insight (the gift of interpreting the divine will and purpose); to another the ability to discern and distinguish between [the utterances of true] spirits [and false ones], to another various kinds of [unknown] tongues, to another the ability to interpret [such] tongues.

11 All these [gifts, achievements, abilities] are inspired and brought to pass by one and the same [Holy] Spirit, Who apportions to each person individually [exactly] as He chooses.

12 For just as the body is a unity and yet has many parts, and all the parts, though many, form [only] one body, so it is with Christ (the Messiah, the Anointed One).

Romans 12 states:

6 Having gifts (faculties, talents, qualities) that differ according to the grace given us, let us use them: [He whose gift is] prophecy, [let him prophesy] according to the proportion of his faith;

7 [He whose gift is] practical service, let him give himself to serving; he who teaches, to his teaching;

8 He who exhorts (encourages), to his exhortation; he who contributes, let him do it in simplicity and liberality; he who gives aid and superintends, with zeal and singleness of mind;

he who does acts of mercy, with genuine cheerfulness and joyful eagerness.

Ephesians 4 states:

He Who descended is the [very] same as He Who also has ascended high above all the heavens, that He [His presence] might fill all things (the whole universe, from the lowest to the highest).

11 And His gifts were [varied; He Himself appointed and gave men to us] some to be apostles (special messengers), some prophets (inspired preachers and expounders), some evangelists (preachers of the Gospel, traveling missionaries), some pastors (shepherds of His flock) and teachers.

If you have lost sight of your dream or never really had any dreams for yourself there is still time for you to go up in life. *"You can do all things through Christ who strengthens you"* (Philippians 4:13*)*. You can even dream again! Even after a divorce or separation you can still dream again. Even after your child has left home in rebellion, you can still dream. Even after your layoff, you can still dream. Even after a tragic accident that has left you with an amputation, you can still dream. Even after the doctor has declared there is no hope for a cure, you can still dream.

Dream of becoming, as Pastor Rachael Campbell

says, a part of something bigger than yourself. Dream of doing something that can benefit someone else. Dream of blooming into your future destiny. God has more in store for all of you so continue to or begin to adore Him.

Chapter 4

Come Up Here!

Another way that you can flourish in life is to climb high in your perspective of both yourself and your life. Go up with the Father and look at your activities from the angle that God sees them. Go up and get a God view of yourself so to speak.

Every year New Life Providence Church in Virginia Beach, Virginia has a Woman's DNA Conference. This conference is a weekend filled with fiery in God's face worship and solid teaching on topics that make you get in touch with your identity. It was at this conference where I had to face the image of myself that I had gained in my lifetime based solely on my circumstances, my upbringing, and what I had been told compared to how God saw me.

What it boils down to is that when you learn to spend time with God, He will give you the vision that He has for you. Worship Leader Kim Walker described it best when she stated, *"There is a perfect mold in God's heart for you."* God formed you and no one can fit in that little spot or mold in God's heart but you! He placed something in your DNA that your parents could not give you even if they tried. It is up to you to search it out and tap into it.

Everyone at this conference was either a Ruth or a Naomi. Some of you know the story like clock-ward, but be patient with me as I describe it briefly for those who do not. Ruth followed her mother-in-law Naomi after the death of her husband. Ruth declared that wherever Naomi went she would follow instead of going her own way. I believe that Ruth had enough wisdom to know that Naomi could teach her things in life. I believe that she was willing to follow Naomi's instructions as Naomi followed the instructions of her God.

As a result of Ruth's obedience she married Boaz, who was a wealthy man in the community that watched her work diligently. In the first book of Matthew Ruth is mentioned as a part of the genealogy of our Lord and Savior Jesus Christ. What an honor for such a sacrifice! So at this conference you are either learning as Ruth who you are and which path you are to take in life or you are taking the time to impart knowledge, confidence, and the truth of who God says a young women is as a Naomi. I believe this conference is so beneficial because the Bible states that the older women are to teach the younger women things about life.

At this same church, Pastor Dan Beckons preached a sermon entitled, *"Come up Here!"* In this message he encouraged the congregation to come up so that we can look down at our lives from a different perspective. He further ministered that we can go up to the Father, out of our emotions, dirt and miry clay to where we could hear God speaking. When you go up to the Father not only will you see yourself differently but you will also get the revelation that God is indeed still on the throne. If your husband, mother, or father has passed, God is still on the throne. If your business has gone bankrupt, God is still on the throne. If you have pursued a dream in the past and failed, God is still on the throne. If you have to make a decision to let go of a relationship that you know will only lead to disaster even though you do not want to be alone; God is still on the throne.

As long as God is still on the throne you can still go to him and make your request known. Esther fasted for three days and went before the king to make her request known. I wonder what would happen in our lives if we carved out three days from our hectic schedules to fast and pray. What results could we possibly have in our lives?

In Matthew Chapter 8 verses 24 and 25, Jesus touched a blind man and he saw everything clearly. What would you see about yourself if you went to Him and saw everything from His perspective? Maybe you would see that for a major portion of your life you have believed the lie that you are not smart, because you were compared to a sibling growing up. But the truth of the matter is you have applied every bit of knowledge that you have gained in your lifetime and God is calling you to write a book or start a blog. Maybe you have believed the lie that God is not real or if He is real He certainly is not concerned with you. The truth is He is so madly in love with you that He allowed you to pick up this book, which you really were not even interested in reading, to know that He has not stopped pursuing you.

I believe that God is saying to you today, "Come up here and see what I have for you. Come up hear and see how that one decision can either positively or negatively affect not only your life, but also that of your future generations." In Revelation Chapter 4 John saw the heavenly worship scene of God's throne in Heaven. Revelation 4

> 4 After this I looked, and behold, a door standing open in heaven! And the first voice which I had heard addressing me like [the calling of] a war trumpet said, Come up here, and I will show you what must take place in the future.
> 2 At once I came under the [Holy] Spirit's power, and behold, a throne stood in heaven, with One seated on the throne!
> 3 And He Who sat there appeared like [the crystalline brightness of] jasper and [the fiery] sardius, and encircling the throne there was a halo that looked like [a rainbow of] emerald.
> 4 Twenty-four other thrones surrounded the throne,

and seated on these thrones were twenty-four elders the members of the heavenly Sanhedrin), arrayed in white clothing, with crowns of gold upon their heads.

5 Out from the throne came flashes of lightning and rumblings and peals of thunder, and in front of the throne seven blazing torches burned, which are the seven Spirits of God [the sevenfold Holy Spirit];

6 And in front of the throne there was also what looked like a transparent glassy sea, as if of crystal. And around the throne, in the center at each side of the throne, were four living creatures (beings) who were full of eyes in front and behind [with intelligence as to what is before and at the rear of them].

7 The first living creature (being) was like a lion, the second living creature like an ox, the third living creature had the face of a man, and the fourth living creature [was] like a flying eagle.

8 And the four living creatures, individually having six wings, were full of eyes all over and within [underneath their wings]; and day and night they never stop saying, Holy, holy, holy is the Lord God Almighty (Omnipotent),Who was and Who is and Who is to come.

9 And whenever the living creatures offer glory and honor and thanksgiving to Him Who sits on the throne, Who lives forever and ever (through the eternities of the eternities),

10 The twenty-four elders (the members of the heavenly Sanhedrin) fall prostrate before Him Who is sitting on the throne, and they worship Him Who lives forever and ever; and they throw down their crowns before the throne, crying out,

11 Worthy are You, our Lord and God, to receive the glory and the honor and dominion, for You created all things; by Your will they were [brought into being] and were created.

What vision does God desire to show you? Seek him in worship today and prepare yourself for the beautiful journey that He has prepared for you. Join the angels in singing the praises of Holy Holy Holy!!! After you have praised and worshiped Him, lie prostrate and listen to what He has to say to you.

Just imagine how you could change the dynamics of the women in your family if you would carve time out to go up to your heavenly father and get to know more about Him. Get to know more about what is in your DNA. Get to know more about who you are and who you were created to be from God's point of view.

Chapter 5

While You're Down There, Sow There!

If we would all be honest, we would realize that we are all traveling to a place called *"there"* in life. None of us have arrived; I certainly do not have it altogether. I am believing God on a daily basis to help me achieve every goal that I have for myself, and for Him to help me do my part to mend every broken relationship in my life as well. The hard part is instead of living in discouragement when things do not go as planned; to take action to continue to sow in whatever place I have found myself in life.

The Bible talks a lot about sowing and reaping and seed time and harvest. The Bible states that, *"Whatsoever a man sows that he will also reap"* (Galatians 6:7). "Those *who sow in tears will reap in joy"* (Psalm 126:5). Think about what would possibly harvest or manifest in your life if you were to begin to sow into your life and into others.

A lot of emphasis is placed on sowing and reaping in the area of finance. And trust me, I completely understand why. I have tried tithing and I have tried not tithing because I thought I did not have enough. Tithing is the best way to go. As a matter of fact, the very first time I paid my tithes I was attending a church were the pastor did not believe in tithes as he said it was a part of the Old Testament. At this time I was simply beginning to read the Bible, listen to televangelists, and I was simply compelled to do it. The lady that was collecting the offering made a big deal about the amount I put on the table with an announcement and clapping of hands. I was so embarrassed. I did not do it for any type of glory; I simply wanted to do as the word stated. Well in this season of my life I was praying for a strong church home and to be connected with strong believers. That very next Sunday I was invited to a church that became my church home for a little over five years.

It was at this place where I learned what worship was and how to enter into His presence. I have always acquainted my obedience of stepping out to pay my tithes even in a church where it was not taught, to being placed strategically by the hand of God in a place where I received strong teaching and discipleship. Now I could be wrong, but that has always been my take on it.

When I first read or reread the scripture, *"Those who sow in tears will reap with joy"* it was as if the words on the page were literally screaming at me. Sometimes you cry about things and you feel as if nobody cares or even knows why the tears are falling from your eyes. I am here to remind you that not one tear drop has gone unnoticed. Not only has God seen you cry but He has bottled up every single one of your tears and will soon pour them back on you as bountiful showers of blessings that will enable your garden of life to grow vigorously.

Some of you may be wondering well if God knew about my pain, where was He or why didn't He intervene to stop or prevent the event that led to my tears. I understand your frustration. I asked God those same questions. His response was, "I was right there with you. When you hurt I hurt. As a matter of fact I knew you were going to have to experience that pain that is why I choose to not come off of that cross. I knew you were going to need somebody to trust and look up to. Thank you for believing in me." Maybe you have cried tears of frustration due to your own poor choices. If so, then always remember Jesus is not ashamed to call you his sister just because you have done something wrong. So go to Him and ask for forgiveness and break forth into your season of development.

No matter what place you have landed in life I believe that it is time for you to begin to prepare yourself for the harvest that is about to be manifested in your life. I believe that God has something so magnificent for you. 1Corinthians 2: 9 states, *"Eyes have not seen, nor ears heard, nor has it entered into the heart of man the things which God has prepared for those who love Him."*

You must continue to sow with your time, money, talents, and thoughts. You must continue to sow because your harvest is near. At any moment now, you never know which seed you sow will begin to sprout out and blossom. 1 Corinthians 3:6-8 states, *"I planted, Apollo's watered, but God gave the increase. So then neither he who plants is anything, nor he who waters, but God who gives the increase. Now he who plants and he who waters are one, and each one will receive his own reward according to his own labor."*

For instance if you have a coworker, neighbor, or friend that just seems incorrigible when it comes to witnessing to, all you have to do is remember that you are simply responsible for sowing the seeds. Continue to sow your seed of a warm smile, or kind affirmations, or complements and others will come as directed by God to water the seeds that you sow. You are simply preparing the soil in their hearts for growth and development.

Some of you may have raised your children in the ways of the Lord but they presently seem to be living as if they never knew anything about the gospel of Jesus. I say hold fast to the notion that you planted the best seed that can be sown that is the seed of the Word of God. The Bible states that, *"His Word will not return unto Him void."* Stand fast that the seed of life will override the power of darkness that desires to choke out the greatness. And even if you are just beginning to learn the word and proclaim it over your children I believe with you that your child will prosper. In the end we win!

I want to admonish you today to prepare the very soil in your life for growth. Just as a gardener must till the soil before harvest time approaches, you must begin to till the things and the qualities that make up the essence of your life. For some of you it could simply be cleaning your natural house or possessions as you believe God for new or more productive things such as buildings, businesses, or appliances. For some of you it may be the tilling of your current relationships as you believe God for a season of new friendships. Yes, that may mean that you need to stop contacting Mr. Tae Diggs lookalike so that the man that God has destined for you can begin to look for you. Yes, this may mean you have to end your weekly phone gossip chats with the woman that has been your best friend since grade school. Truth be told, you cannot make any new friends as long as you are still known to be connected to the gossip queen.

It can be so difficult to weed out the people that we already know deep down in our hearts are not good for our future. But just as a gardener toils to pull out the weeds in order to make room for the beautiful fruits and flowers that are to come we must begin to toil to pull out the weeds of unfruitful friendships from our lives. I believe that as we begin this process in due time we will begin to see our lives full of people that share our hearts desires. I believe we will begin to see our lives full of people that have our best interest at hand and that we can in return be a blessing to as well.

No matter what state or condition of life you are presently in God will allow you to have an encounter with his Holy Spirit that will enable your growth to take place. Maybe you are in a place in life right now where your soil seems as if it is just unmanageable. It seems more like dried up clay than soil. Well I have news for you. In the book of Isaiah it is declared that God will even allow rivers to grow in your desert places. So whatever area of life has caused you grief or turmoil for years on end, no worries, God has a plan to prosper you right in the middle of it all. Jeremiah 17:7-8 of the Message Bible states, *"But blessed is the man who trusts me, God, the woman who sticks with God. They're like trees replanted in Eden, putting down roots near the rivers- Never a worry through the hottest of summers, never dropping a leaf, Serene and calm through droughts, bearing fresh fruit every season"*(Jeremiah 17: 7-8).

"Behold, I will do a new thing. Now it shall spring forth; shall you not know it? I will even make a road in the wilderness and rivers in the desert" (Isaiah 43:19). Just imagine how you would feel if you had been walking in a hot dry desert for days, weeks, maybe even months, or years. Imagine how you would feel if you were lost on an unfamiliar highway with no navigation. Now imagine the elatedness your soul would experience. Well get ready because I believe you will experience these emotions as your life will flourish.

Go ahead and prepare your soil/soul for supernatural growth. Psalm 92:12 states that the righteous will flourish like a palm tree. Proverbs 11:28 states to not trust in riches because they will fall but the righteous will thrive (or flourish) like a green leaf. Psalm 1:3 states, *"He shall a like a tree planted by the rivers of water, that brings forth its fruit in its season, whose leaf also shall not wither, and whatever he does shall prosper."*

"The wilderness and the solitary place shall be glad for them; and the desert shall rejoice, and blossom as the rose" (Isaiah 35:1). When a rose blossoms the petals spread. When the petals spread the aroma gets stronger. Leave your desert place deserted forever and blossom with the new mercies God is bestowing upon you. As you blossom your sphere of influence will continue to grow and your impact on others will become stronger. My prayer is that as we continue to flourish in life that we will also flourish in our spiritual life of prayer, praise, and worship. I pray that the aroma of our worship will get stronger and sweeter to our Father God. And as the late Nelson Mandela so eloquently stated, *"Let your greatness blossom."*

ABOUT THE AUTHOR

KATESHA MELODY WALKER HARRELL

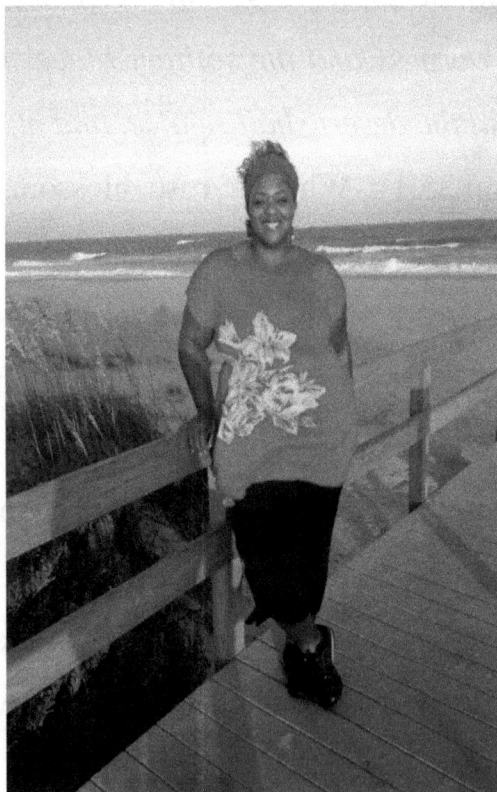

Katesha Melody Walker Harrell has a Bachelor's Degree in English and Middle Grades Education. She is a mother and a Middle Grades Language Arts and Social Studies Teacher.